Author: Dr Desre Coertze
Published in 2017
Published by: Africa Integrated Media

To order copies please go to:
www.IntoStillness.net

Copyright © 2017 by Dr Desre Coertze

All rights reserved. No part of this publication may be reproduced, distributed, or transmitted in any form or by any means, including photocopying, recording, or other electronic or mechanical methods, without the prior written permission of the publisher, except in the case of quotations embodied in reviews and certain other noncommercial uses permitted by copyright law. Any quotations in reviews and certain other noncommercial uses must credit the book and author as the source.

For permission requests, please write to the publisher, addressed at the email addresses below:

Info@knowledge-executive.com and
lifebetweenlives@webmail.co.za

Edition 01

ISBN: 978-0-620-77967-8

Into Stillness

Acknowledgements

Gratitude is due to the many spiritual students for sharing the unfolding of this journey, their pertinent questions, enthusiasm, and willingness to step into the unknown and to:

Mark Angus for the diligence required to prepare and edit the manuscript.

Biddie Breeds and Janice Grace for proofreading and their generosity of spirit.

Sean Copping-Rice for the creative development and layout of the manuscript.

Into Stillness

Prologue

All of Creation came from infinity and perfection long ago in the memory of Existence Itself. Physical and non-physical were the expressions of this creation. Aspects of the physical, expressed as the human experience, became separated therefrom as part of a journey of awakening and would unfold as a discovery and as the remembrance of Who They Really Are; God expressed; One. This journey of the awakening of consciousness would entail many experiences over which aspects of The Absolute would remember and awaken to itself.

One such expression entered the human experience being born in South Africa. Raised in the conservative ways of her ancestors, the girl learned of this world through surviving cancer, losing her father and then her primary family before she could write her name.

The will to overcome and survive and the gift of a good intellect afforded her the courage and strength to pull through. In this she discovered what it meant to be and do things for herself while opening her heart to others who were also in suffering. The encounter with cancer cost her her innocence and outer beauty. She stood on the outside looking in, and her own observation, that she was different in more ways than one, became her reality. She became aware of a deep longing that was guiding her inwards. A longing for God, untainted, unchangeable and eternal, would become her fuel for life. The girl learned the ways of the intellect through the limited and pre-scribed government school system, university and her experiences as qualified social worker.

All the while, she had memories, insights and knowings from other worlds, other places of learning and other lifetimes. Her ability to know and see beyond the obvious was very strong and others would seek her counsel for her clarity and ability to accept and deeply connect with what and who was in front of her.

As the girl walked in different worlds simultaneously and cumulatively, an inner wisdom beyond the intellect surfaced which would guide her in times of trouble and suffering.

Over time she expanded her knowledge, deepening her understanding of the nature of the human experience through studying Transpersonal Psychology, Hypnosis, and Metaphysics - none of which surpassed her growing inner knowing and awakening memories that there is only One.

The expression of the Absolute that was "she" was different from anybody that she knew and yet paradoxically the same. She became a loner, set apart from culture, religion and those sharing her life, resulting in others calling her strange. Yet she was a relentless searcher for answers to her questions and inner conflicts; that which she knew - and that which she encountered in the world - differed. For most of her adult life she explored the scriptures of numerous religions, the truths of enlightened ones and spiritual teachers from different times, cultures and tongues, only to discover that there is no absolute truth, that there is no 'map to freedom from suffering' and that they could only point her to the Self. Her own Truth.

She realised over time that Who She Really Is was the limitless inner sky that had always been inside her, a Presence, a voice that spoke without words that wisely guided her and others. Inner peace, stillness and wisdom were not only her Truth but Who She Was - the Universe having a human experience. God expressed as human.

Over the years, while on her own inner path, others who were also beginning to remember Who They Really Are, would sit with her and listen, learn and share. In these times they knowingly and unknowingly inspired her and their contributions disappeared in her and her being.

The girl (now a women) knew that it was Life's expression as her who guided and helped others to remember what she had come to remember: That they were not their thoughts, minds or bodies; that they were not male or female, Hindu, Christian or Muslim, black or white, rich or poor, good or bad. As she came to know, she pointed them to their essence: that which cannot be named. As she guided them, so it was for her.

In time, the longing that she carried for the Divine everywhere and over lifetimes, in her eyes and heart, was answered. In the decent into Nothingness, in days of intense despair when she had thought that she was forsaken by Life itself, she discovered with absolute clarity that there was no God and no her. In the illusive space between God and her, "the self", "me", "I", was lost. There was no longer anyone to achieve or anyone to fail. There was only Stillness, only God. There were no thoughts, no words, no understanding. It was impossible to express what the stillness, spaciousness and the Presence was. It just was.

In the days and weeks that followed, the stillness persisted and deepened. There was no-one there, no personal will; the physical body went about automatically under the gentle Will of the Presence. What unfolded in every moment became self-evident. There were no thoughts, just an all-encompassing knowing. The physical body carried far more energy than ever before. The adjustment to ordinary life was challenging as there was difficulty in communication and expression. All previous motivations disappeared and with it all fear and anxiety. There was nothing more to seek, as everything was experienced as "it is what it is".

Slowly the body adjusted to the high energy levels and in the place of the personal self or ego-mind was only a silent witness to these phenomena and life. It was clear that life would continue to unfold, despite of the illusion of the personal self. All along there was only God.

At times an intensified experience of expandedness would occur, which made it difficult to function and return to everyday activities. In these times all boundaries between here and there, then and now, or separation disappeared.

The inner silence, the strength of the Presence continued to grow and life was no longer personal. The personal Self had become an instrument of the Divine Presence. This state of consciousness continues to unfold and still does today.

The ability to share her experiences with others happened automatically; nothing but the expression of Consciousness itself. The body and intellect was available, willing and accepting of What Is.

Prologue

In time a passion and dedication arose to share with those who would be ready to remember. She started writing down that which would arise in the silence.

The contemplations and insights were reminders for awaking to a new conscious way of living. There was the knowing that nothing that arose in the silence - nothing that was written down and shared - could add anything to anybody. It only served as reminders to readers of that which separated them from the truth of WHO THEY REALLY ARE and already knew within themselves.

The writings have no specific order of importance or theme but serve as reminders on the inner path. To be reminiscent that spiritual awakening is Self-awakening and that no one can save another from suffering, but themselves. No teacher, no book, no process, no workshop, no ritual or ceremony can, or may. Everybody has to find their own path and walk it. It is the greatest privilege and opportunity of the human experience and these reminders merely serve as guidelines.

Once the reminders were shared with others, the same question was asked more than once: "Why not write a book?" The reminders could then be contemplated on over and again and would serve as a gift to those who are starting to remember.

The knowing was there that when it was time, the inspiration and guidance would be there, and when it happened, she reached for her laptop and created a compilation of that which was spoken in the silence, one teacher, one learner, in a world of others. She knew that between the written words, beyond all the concepts, readers would find their truth.

For the writings to be reminders and also inspirational, the pages of the book are not numbered. In that way it would be useful for readers to hold a question in their mind, randomly open the book, and read the reminder on which their eyes would first alight. They would find what they needed most, in that moment, right in front of them.

The book could also be used as a guide for life's journey - something to live with, to return to over and again; to contemplate on. Through contemplating on the insights their hearts would remember.

And so Silence spoke:

Reminders on the Inner Path.

Ever wondered why everything around you seems so chaotic? Mother Earth - and the human race who are one with Her - is in a process of rebirth and unprecedented change. Predicted by ancient prophecies and modern day science, the rebirth for us as humans is about moving from a consciousness of division, greed and destruction to a consciousness of solidarity, cooperation and care. To survive as a species we have no other choice but to wake up to Who We Really Are or we will continue to destroy each other, our home and our planet. What is your role in all of this? It starts by becoming aware of your own suffering and the suffering of those around you. It starts with taking the responsibility of becoming the change you desire. It starts with learning the skill of being in the moment - because change can only happen in the NOW. This can be your contribution of a lifetime. Everything else - being financially secure, being successful, being respected, physically attractive, having the ideal relationship, happy children, etc. - is secondary. Are you ready for the change and the opportunity of a lifetime? If so, these words may ring true for you.

Beyond the rat race, beyond the day-to-day striving to make life work, to survive, beyond all trials and tribulations, lies an inner Stillness, a vast, cloudless, eternal sky of wisdom, an Inner Presence. You are That.

Inner peace is not the absence of struggle, but the complete acceptance of uncertainty and confusion as part of the human experience. Suffering happens when you have the desire, or expectation, for things to be different.

The greatest contribution you can make in this lifetime is not to give to the beggar on the street. It is not to rally for any humanitarian course or freedom of any kind. It is also not to be a leader at any level, successful, rich or influential. Your greatest contribution does not lie in giving or doing. It lies in turning inward and finding Inner Peace. Then, whether you give or not, it happens without an agenda and everything and everybody benefits from it.

We often mistake suffering as being hungry, homeless or dying. The suffering of loneliness, fear, being unloved and unwanted is the greatest, the most terrible, suffering. In all suffering, be it your own or another's, do not forget that we are One - we belong to each other.

Reminders on the Inner Path

Human consciousness can be compared to a house with many floors. On the lower floors, consciousness is caught up in separation and the illusion of the self, also the illusion of individual souls. Once consciousness shifts to the higher floors, separation is experienced as an illusion of the mind and then Oneness with All (Enlightenment) unfolds. The illusion of the separate soul disappears and there is the experience of Self – One Soul.

If I step out of the mind - and with it my life story - I see that Presence always surrounds us just as the sky holds everything in it. I experience that Presence in everything, also in my journey of remembering and waking up. Through awareness, through watching, my heart opens and catches the blessings that are there in every moment.

The greatest freedom lies in trusting the Inner Presence and not thoughts, feelings or emotions.

The capacity for love begins with inner stillness, independence, self-sufficiency, and the ability to be alone. Only when we are whole and mature in ourselves are we able to share with others and connect with our 'other Selves'. This is a connection that allows the other complete and absolute freedom to be and to know. When the other goes, one will be as content and happy without them, as one is with them. There is deep understanding that love and happiness cannot be given or taken by others, it has to be found within. If not, it is not love - it might be many other things - but it is not love.

There is something about sitting alone in the dark that always reminds me of how precious the human experience really is, and how much of it is spent on following the lives, thoughts and opinions of others. How often we allow the noise of life to drown out our Inner Voice. How often we forget to sing our own songs, write our own poetry, make our own music, and dance our own dance. How often we forget that we have to find our own way to our own castle. .

A humble "I dont know", remains the most intimate companion on the inner path.

The sole task of all human life is to reunite with our Source, our Selves: Godness.

Reminders on the Inner Path

When you accept that Life doesn't need you, everything changes - you can start flowing with things as they are. Once you understand this, the world takes on a different colour. You are not fighting, you are not pushing; you can feel the music and you start dancing despite of what is in front of you. Sometimes it is hot, sometimes it is cold, sometimes there is joy, sometimes there is sadness - but now everything, every situation, every person brings a message from the whole. Every moment becomes a teacher.

Waiting for other people to act in a certain way, and to be happy themselves, is making your happiness dependent upon something outside of yourself. It is turning your power over to others and allowing them to influence how you feel. Stillness comes from knowing that what you feel is your choice. Everything in life is teaching you about yourself. You can choose peace no matter how others are acting if you take on the opportunity to be responsible for your own emotions.

As you flow with Life, inner acceptance of what is in the moment becomes a natural experience along with spiritual growth. There is no desire to change anything, and there is the realisation, at the deepest level, that nothing is ever out of place. Does it mean that you passively accept your life situations? No. First there is inner acceptance and you realise: "this is what it is"; then you engage fully with what is in front of you. The difference that inner acceptance makes is, when you act, you no longer act from the past. You no longer come from resistance or old programming. Your response and engagement is fresh, authentic and unpredictable.

To be totally accepting means not to quarrel with what is showing up right now. It means not to reject it, or throw it back, or walk away from it. Embrace it, and hold it as if it were your own, because it is your own. You have invited it in, in order to learn something from it. Don't miss the opportunity.

When we live with awareness we can no longer feel that life is happening to us. There is the inner knowing that whatever we are facing at any time fits perfectly into the awakening of our consciousness. Then when we experience a life crisis or challenge, we no longer ask: "How do I get out of it?" or "When will it be done?" Instead we know that the only way through it, is to be willing and available to be changed because of it.

Reminders on the Inner Path

The River of Life flows by itself - despite of us. The human experience is an opportunity to experience the here and now and to discover and live the Absolute in everything and everybody; To BE.

On my journey, I learned that in order to give up the ego-mind, I first had to develop a healthy, mature ego. When the moment came to surrender the personal self, there was nothing to give up but an illusion and I learned that the ego becomes mature through humility. I saw myself as I really was, acknowledging both the light and the shadow in me and not being identified or attached to either. Who I was included all of this, and yet none of it.

The world has no value but the value you give it. The eyes through which you see the world determine the shape of your world. You don't see things as they are - you see things as you are. Your level of consciousness determines your world.

All questions come from the mind. When aware, the answer is very concrete: Wherever you are, whatever is in front of you. It is very important to be in our direct experience in this very moment. Right here and now is where our questions and our incompleteness fall away. Right here is where we find the real answers, the true meaning of our world.

When fully aware, the mind, the body, personality and life roles are experienced as a garment. When not fully aware, we are identified with them, so much so that we believe that is who we are. If the body is beautiful we believe that we are beautiful. If the body is not beautiful we believe that we are not attractive. If we play a certain role in life, being an athlete, artist, teacher, mother or friend, we believe that is who we are. We get identified with the different ways in which we express ourselves in the outer world. This identification has become so strong and so deep that the garment we are wearing ceases to be a garment - we think that we are the garment. This identification is the source of all separation and suffering. We are so much more. We are Life Itself.

Spiritual growth does not happen through staying safe; growth comes from the willingness to leave our world of safety and move into the unknown. As we meet our challenges, it strengthens us by forcing us to grow. We must be willing to take up responsibility for our own happiness and our own suffering - we can no longer be victims or be passive. We must be willing to step out of the familiar and expected and confront the challenge of uncertainty. When willing to face the unknown - to be courageous - we do not get "bogged" down by obstacles. We do not lose our direction when we are challenged, but go forth with trust and strength. Strength in the eye of the storm can only be earned through experience.

Many spiritual practices, especially those orientated towards spiritual awakening, advise that the (little) self should be given up, to surrender to a master, a guru, or a particular concept of God. While it is important to give up attachments, what is really called for is to dissolve into the Divine. To become one with the Divine is not to abandon the Self, but to REALISE that divine consciousness is who the Self really is. We do not lose our sense of self, we reframe it. The Self then includes the All. This is our final transcendence into Oneness.

Consciousness is our means of travel as human beings. It is that which is reading these words right now, sorting them out, making sense of them. That which drew you to this book, chose your partner, lives your daily life. It is that which sees, hears, remembers, feels, thinks, and moves your body through its daily activities.

The separation of spirituality from the rest of our lives leaves us spiritually homeless. For many spiritual students, the spiritual journey is practiced and divorced from ordinary day-to-day human life. Enlightenment is sought by denying the basic nature of their biological existence. Yet denying our physical existence in order to reach unity with all is a contradiction steeped in dualistic thinking, which can never lead us to wholeness.

All of Life is an expression of God; everything in existence has its source in the Transcendent - God is Life. It is forever where we are and forever who we are; it is All. Therefore all paths of spiritual growth, any framework, any inner journey, are fit for uniting with the Absolute. There is NO exclusive map, no exclusive truth to Oneness with ALL. The purpose of all spiritual work, the sole purpose of the human experience, is to grow into unity with ALL, which is a state of consciousness where we experience being One with the Infinite. This is Enlightenment or Self-realisation.

The inward journey can be compared to a bridge, it is about connection. The two ends of the bridge connect the individual self with the universal Self. Our work on this journey is to discover the Divine and then LIVE the Divine through manifesting divinity in our bodies and actions and so transform the world. When the discovery of the Divine is made we see divinity in everything and everybody and in all its infinite arrangements in the physical world. Spiritual work is about stretching to connect the limited with the infinite, while still retaining both qualities. It is through that stretch that we grow.

We are not just passing through on earth; we are here on serious business. We are here to discover our true Being. The discovery of what is REAL is not a mass action but a lone journey to remember that we are not the body, emotions, intellect or our life situations. We are limitless inner peace, love and intelligence.

Reminders on the Inner Path

If you are passionate and committed to reach Self-Realisation then the ego-mind and its internal dialogue should be transcended. Make a decision to become aware of your need to control, your need for approval and your need to judge. Those are the main strategies of the ego which keeps the illusion of 'me' or ‹i› in place.

No two people have the same reality, only partially shared realities. That implies that a personal opinion or perception is just what it says: a personal interpretation of a personal reality. A deep understanding of this insight can prevent conflict in relationships and motivate people to focus on that which is shared, or to look in the direction of a solution. You are the only one that creates your reality.

The petty concerns that occupy the bulk of our life often distract us from remembering who we truly are beneath the careers, cars, the children and the clothes. It is important to know that we are the Divine expressed as humans, and that there is a deeper meaning to life that underlies all of Existence. Stripping ordinary day-to-day living of its spiritual meaning leaves many people without purpose or direction. Our purpose is indeed awakening to Oneness of All but, we must be fully grounded in our "humanness" and day-to-day life, for it facilitates our greatest teachings, moment by moment.

Realising that there is no absolute Truth was a turning point for Buddha on his journey to Self-Realisation. As spiritual students we now greatly benefit from this knowing - that truth is only relative and not absolute. All truth is only so within a certain level of consciousness. For instance, to forgive is commendable at a certain level of consciousness, but with deepened awareness, one sees that there is actually nothing to forgive as there is no "other" to be forgiven. Everyone's ego-mind is equally unreal, including one's own. Perception is not reality, it is simply a personal interpretation of what is.

For many committed and passionate spiritual students, years of inner struggle, suffering and seemingly futile spiritual practice and strife can often cultivate a state of despair. This continues until there is the realisation that reason and intellect are too frail for the formidable task of finding the Ultimate/The Infinite. In a stunning moment the mind reaches a final agonizing point of defeat and surrenders itself to an all-encompassing awareness, becoming silent and still as the promised essence of All That Is. Enlightenment and self-realisation is born in a moment of the deepest possible despair; the death of the ego-mind followed by total surrender and moments of the most beautiful grace. It cannot be willed by the ego/self.

When we are in anger, the capacity to observe is almost entirely lost. And the fact is that the capacity to observe is never more needed than when we are angry. The irony is when the watcher is in place, when we are aware there is no anger, and vice-versa. Both cannot be present at the same time. If a person who is angry becomes interested in observing, anger will disappear. One who is aware will find it difficult to fight. In order to fight one has to be unaware.

We came from infinity and perfection long ago in the memory of the Infinite Source. In time we became separated from this Source. This wrenching separation is what we now experience, this is our reality. The fact is, in our essence, in our Being, we have never left our Source. But our day-to-day experience tells us otherwise. Our inexpressible driving desire for happiness, fulfilment, and contentment, tell us otherwise. We do not know exactly what we seek, but we know that it is the Nameless, that which we cannot define. If we did give it a name, it might be God. We seek it where we can - mostly outside ourselves in work, relationships, financial security, religion - whatever and wherever our world facilitates for us. The Truth is that the route, the journey and the goal is within us.

Creation/God has no agenda for, or expectations of us. What we want for ourselves is what Creation wants for us - be it positive or negative. Our level of consciousness determines the choices we make, and the choices we make colour our human experience; either as heaven or hell.

The very effort to "become" is a barrier in all spiritual work. That is because we already carry our highest potential, the Inner Presence within. We don't need to become anything or anybody. We simply need to realise who we are and realise what has always been within us. We merely have be aware, alert, and watchful, and be honest with ourselves about ourselves. This is the only spiritual work ever needed - the rest unfolds naturally.

At daybreak I awaken with the call of a Piet-My-Vrou. After almost a week of wind and dust, the sky is covered with the promise of rain. In me, is the awareness of the desire for rain, for enough water for humans, animals, and nature, and for the drought to be over. With this awareness, there is a return to inner stillness and the knowing that there can be no spring without a long, dry winter. There can be no appreciation for rain without the experience of drought. It is what it is, and my heart is filled with a deep gratitude for the human experience.

We face the unknown in every moment. The past is no more and the future has yet to come into being. The future is unpredictable, in every moment we stand at the door of the unpredictable. In every moment the unknown is our guest and anything can happen. If the unknown is so familiar to us, then why fear tomorrow, why fear change, why the resistance?

Acceptance of what is, is the greatest teacher for conflict, strife and suffering. Acceptance comes from the realisation that every moment - everything and everybody - serves a purpose. It comes with the humility that we will not understand all events and circumstances. Acceptance is an inner phenomenon and is never passive. It displays a deep trust that EVERYTHING serves ALL. Most important is the realisation that all spiritual progress- acceptance included - is due to Life/God and not the result of one's own personal endeavours.

There is only one reason for focusing on 'becoming better' or 'more successful' or 'more aware'. The reason is that we spend most of our lives dwelling on what was, what is not, and what might have been.

The best one can do when it rains is to be fully available to the experience and allow it to rain. After all, one has no control over it and if one resists it in any way, the beauty and gratitude of the experience is lost. In the words of Bob Marley: "Some people feel the rain - others just get wet." This, incidentally, is also true about what we call the 'human experience'.

Kindness is the willingness to forgive and overlook. The committed spiritual student resigns from the ego-duties to judge, correct, control, change the world, and express opinions about everything. There is the realisation that each person is merely on their own journey and that one should respect it and allow them to do so. When aware and non-attached, it is easy to observe that most people enjoy the drama of their lives. It is therefore quite helpful to give up efforts to change the world, rally for the less fortunate, and for other causes and sentimentalities. Kindness becomes an act of the heart and one no longer moves from the ego-mind or pain body. One is kind and forgiving without a personal agenda or gain. It simply is what it is.

If you feel incomplete, you alone must fill yourself with love in all your empty, wounded places. Then when you need nothing, you can love another unconditionally without any limitations whatsoever; you can grant them total freedom. Freedom is the basic concept and construct of life everywhere, because freedom is the basic nature of God. The less you need from someone the more you can love them.

Forgiveness is just another word for peace in the language of consciousness.

This is my truth: Love is unconditional; if it is not, then it is not Love. Life is never-ending; it is impossible to die. We are living a miracle of God made human. This we have known all along within our hearts, and it is what our minds keep on denying. This is what consciousness is whispering time and time again, only to be silenced by our bodies and our minds. Yet the refusal to know ourselves as ONE with ALL is what is causing all the pain and suffering in our lives. The Ultimate Truth is: God is found inside!

What function does prayer have in spiritual work? When unaware, prayer is an attempt to 'get' something for the self or others, such as good health, a new car etc. from an 'outer God'. As awareness progresses, the intention to control God/Life is given up and prayer becomes a dedication instead of a request. As awareness increases further from selfishness to selflessness, the quality of communication shifts to a willingness to be a channel or expression of Life/God without trying to specify the 'what' or 'how' it is to be done. Prayer becomes an interaction and an experience - a surrender rather than supplication. As consciousness deepens, further separation and distance between the i and God/Life falls away and an all-encompassing Inner Presence arises which is experienced as an unwavering inner peace and stillness - a voice that speaks without words. This unification affords the shattering of the belief that God exists outside oneself and is referred to as God -or Self- Realisation.

Meditation followed by a cup of tea. Passing time as it comes, looking down at the spring garden, looking up at the promise of rain. How grateful, serene, peaceful and quiet I feel. Aware and in the moment.

Good personhood - or a perfect personality - is commendable but it does not in itself result in a person's highest potential: enlightenment. The idea of being a "good" person often becomes an obstacle in spiritual work simply because it reinforces duality; good versus bad. The path to enlightenment indicates that as much as duality is an illusion, there is no point in trying to perfect it. Therefore, the ego needs to be transcended and seen for the illusion that it is. The possibility of reaching your highest potential is based on committed daily spiritual practice and self-honesty, and not through being a "good" person.

Everything changes when we realise that the human experience is but ONE of the expressions of God.

What inspires people to turn inward? When and how does the 'spiritual will' become activated? The spiritual path is accessed either through awareness or through reaching a point in life where a person is overwhelmed by their life circumstances through suffering. As a result the search for God or the meaning of Life is initiated.

Reminders on the Inner Path

Contentment comes as the infallible result of great acceptances and great humilities. Not trying to make ourselves this or that, but surrendering ourselves to the fullness of life, and letting life express itself as and through us.

Spiritual growth through consciousness is actually uncomplicated and simple. The primary quality is really one of perspective, in that one engages with the human experience, not as a space for gain but as an opportunity for learning.

There are no saints and no sinners; there are only people who are spiritually asleep and people who are spiritually awake. The difference is so small that if one is in the moment - truthful to oneself and aware - all differences disappear.

What does the Self feel like? It is like the ultimate feeling of being home and there is a profound sense of certainty. The unlimited spaciousness dissolves all possibilities of suffering and wanting and there are no thoughts; only a deep 'knowingness'. There is absolutely nothing in the egoic human experience to compare to the stillness and beingness of ALLTHAT IS/GOD. No sacrifice is too great nor effort too much in order to realise the Self, which is your highest potential.

A dedication to the inner path soon brings the realisation that the ego-mind is an illusion and the source of all separation and suffering. In the process we learn that in order to give up the insecure, fearful and emotionally over-sensitive ego; we first have to develop a healthy, mature ego which ultimately surrenders of its own accord.

All spiritual learning is un-learning and is about making the unconscious, conscious while becoming aware of one's programming, conditioning and belief systems – and then dropping them. In the process one discovers that one is not who one thought one was. One is not female or male, nor Hindu, Christian or Muslim, black or white, rich or poor, good or bad. One discovers that Who You Are in essence lies beyond all concepts. Who You Are cannot be named, and is unchangeable and untouched by the human experience. Everything one can ever be or know has always been there, and will always be there. Teaching, therefore, is reminding others that they already know - they just need to turn inward to find it. We are all learners and teachers of Life.

Love cannot be asked for, only given.

All inner resistance is experienced as negativity or suffering in one form or another. ALL SUFFERING IS RESISTANCE.

Reminders on the Inner Path

The human experience is our exercise book, the pages on which we do our mathematics, write our songs and poetry and paint our pictures; the pages on which we write our life stories. Life has NO agenda and no specific outcome for our physical experiences, so we are also free to write nonsense, or lies, or tear the pages. What is important is not to confuse Who We Really Are with what we do in the exercise book. It is not Reality, only an EXERCISE, an expression. It is not reality, although we can choose to make it our reality if we wish to.

We are all here as expressions of the Divine, of Life Itself, to express our own unique colour and fragrance of Life. Each of us has an important piece to express in the picture of Life. When we are stuck in the ego-mind and the past - when we resist our story or ourselves - we perpetuate our own suffering and that of others in every moment, every day, every week and every year; it is impossible to become aware of our inner divinity and how to extract the ingredients we need to live it. All of our dramas and each experience - the parts of ourselves that we love and the parts that we resist - are what make us unique expressions of Life. Some of us are expressed as centre parts of the picture, some of us as the peripheral parts. There is no other piece of the "picture of Life" like you. Your unique expression is there at birth and every day thereafter. So whatever your story is - wherever you find yourself right now - know that there are NO mistakes in life - only expressions of Life itself.

The desire for peace and the end of suffering and pain is a reflection of one's own programming and conditioning. One suffers because of these attitudes and belief systems and not because of what is happening in the world. External situations simply trigger one's own unresolved personal pain and with it the judgments of what is right and wrong - what is pain and what is suffering. Suffering or pain is therefore an interpretation, a meaning the mind gives to a situation. It implies a judgment formed by the mind's personal perception of it to be good, bad, desired or undesired. What is our work as spiritual students? Stop trying to understand, control or change the world. Be fully with what is, and there will be nothing but an experience. Not good, not bad, not right, not wrong - just an experience.

How do you know that you are growing spiritually? How do you know that you are remembering more of Who You Really Are? There are many indications, and here are but three of the most obvious: 1) Less thinking. Not because of the fact that the nature of the mind has changed (which is not possible) but when in the now - when aware - the ego- mind is transcended, and there are periods of no thinking.
2) Secondly, one's day-to-day life becomes easier. Once one gives attention and consciously engages with one's past and one's pain, the way one relates to life changes. Life's challenges will always be there, but now you are no longer overwhelmed or "fazed" by them.
3) Thirdly, an inner peace and stillness arises that is not disturbed by the outer world - no matter what occurs.

Reminders on the Inner Path

The ego-mind hankers to be somebody, to stand out, to be different, to be seen, to be an achiever, to be special, to be extraordinary. No matter what is achieved in the outer world it is still ordinary, because whatever is achieved in the outer world comes and goes. Extra-ordinariness starts only when there is NO yearning for extra-ordinariness. Then the journey has started and the seed for inner peace has sprouted.

The ego-mind can only position itself as either the victim or the perpetrator; the one that causes something, or the one to whom something is done. Beyond the ego there is no object or subject and therefore, there is no relationship to explain. In transcending the limitations of the illusive world that the ego creates it is helpful to to cease having OPINIONS about ANYTHING. All opinions are vanities; they are based on duality and tend to reinforce this. Once one becomes aware of this it becomes obvious that almost every thought is an opinion.

You can decide in advance how you choose to experience your day: as a victim, with insecurity, fear, irritation, or stress, or with gratitude, humility, joy and creativity? You get to choose your experience of every moment – no matter what the moment presents. You decide consciously or unconsciously who you are in every moment.

There are many ways to reach Self-Realisation but NO easy way. It cannot be given by somebody or something. It is and will always remain our own responsibility. The common denominator on the journey is making our own darkness conscious. The central task is that of awareness. This is our first and final task. Knowing, accepting, and embracing our own darkness is the secret door to our inner divinity.

It is not true that the up cycles in life are "good" and the down cycles are "bad". This judgment only exists in the human ego-mind. Growth is usually considered to be positive, but nothing can grow forever - not even a business, relationship, career, nation or economy. Dissolution is needed for growth to happen. Our down cycles are absolutely essential for spiritual growth and realisation because it is through failure, pain, and loss that we are drawn to spiritual work - or return to it. What is our work as spiritual students? Learn to live with insecurity. Accept the ups and downs of life as it is NEVER going to change. It is the very nature of the dualistic reality that we are living in for now. Realise that your ONLY security lies in your ability to flow with life. Find the courage to face what is in front of you, moment by moment.

Reminders on the Inner Path

Life itself knows no centre, no right or wrong, and no drama. The ego-mind is the "problem creator". It needs problems, tension and drama, and because of this need, the outer world is blamed for the dilemmas it creates. The ego blames other people, lack of time, circumstances and life for the unhappiness, pressure, and suffering it creates. Where there is conflict, stress and tension there is ego. If one understands this deeply the attraction and need for drama can be dropped. One CAN choose to be aware, to see the ego-mind and loose the interest in drama. One can CHOOSE to live in the moment - where the ego-mind is not. If you decide otherwise it is your choice of course. As I see it, life is a gift that one CHOOSES and wherein one decides to be alive. I chose to stop fooling myself years ago and I chose life. What do you choose, ego and its dramas, or awareness and inner peace?

If we look closely at our lives, we will see that we have always had whatever we have needed in order to get to the next moment, and ultimately, to bring us here, where we are right now. The evidence of this fact is that we ARE here and that clearly we have needed nothing more. We might have WANTED something more, but we have NEEDED nothing more. ALL OUR NEEDS HAVE BEEN MET. This is because there is only ONE OF US, and there is NO separation between us.

Does spiritual commitment mean one has to give up the world? No, of course not. It means merely that worldly life needs to be re-conceptualized, restructured and perceived differently. It is not the outer world that is the problem or that causes suffering, but one's attachment to it along with one's programming and conditioning. Once the ego-mind collapses the outer world is experienced as it is: joyous and benevolent.

No one can force you to learn and grow - you will learn and grow when you want to. The want to learn is afforded by your level of consciousness and before you learn, something important will be at risk.

It is impossible to live without God/The Ultimate/Life. "Without God" is not a state in which we can EVER find ourselves. How do we LIVE this truth? We can start by listening to our inner guidance.

Spiritual surrender, the key to Self-Awakening, is a constant process of NOT resisting or clinging to the moment but instead continuously allowing it or flowing with it. The attention is focused on allowing the moment to come and go and not on the "what" that is being experienced.

Unconditional love cannot be learned, simply because it is our very nature obscured by the ego. The way that we reach into our innate ability to love all and everything without condition is to become aware and to be honest with ourselves about how unloving, unkind, and conditional we are. All other attempts are in vain.

Spiritual practice does not only mean meditation, attending a circle or workshop, process or retreat when your outer world schedule allows it. It is a way of living - a DEVOTION to Life Itself. It is finding the heart of Life in every moment, whatever one is doing - meditating, eating, working, playing or driving in rush hour traffic. It is about how fully we engage with every situation and every relationship. It is about self-honesty in every moment, observing oneself, and taking responsibility for the change one desires.

In every moment we have a choice to be clear and compassionate or to be distracted, or obstinate and unaware. In every moment we have the choice to allow every person and every situation to transform us.

What is usually implied by the concept "spiritual ego or pride" is the result of the illusion that there is a personal self that is doing the spiritual work. All spiritual interest, commitment and work is the result of the Self not the self. The spiritual ego is thwarted by surrender, humility, and gratitude.

When we step back far enough to see the design, to see the beauty of the intricate and delicate weavings in the fabric of Life, we are filled with gratitude! We know that nothing occurs in life by chance. Nothing takes place without producing the opportunity for real and lasting benefit to ALL.

When inwardly totally free, one has no yearning to be outwardly free. One is capable of accepting life as it is and making the necessary compromises when life asks for it.

Who am I? Who do I choose to be? These are the most important questions to consider as we journey through Life. These are the only questions that matter and this is what we are using to decide and direct our lives in every moment - not to find out - to decide. For Life is not a process of discovery, it is a process of creation.

We determine what something means and we give it meaning. Until we decide what something means, it has NO meaning at all. Remember this deeply - we give meaning to everything in life. When unaware, the meaning will unconsciously come from our conditioning, programming and suffering - our past. When aware, we can consciously choose what meaning we want to give to every moment.

Reminders on the Inner Path

God is not just present everywhere, there is nothing but God. What we experience as our world is not a creation of God, but God itself. The Creator and Creation are one and the same. God is beyond perception and duality and therefore, beyond good and bad, right or wrong, win or lose, here or there. The degree to which the nature of God is realised varies markedly from one person to another and is dependant on one's level of consciousness. Once the illusion of the ego or the self collapses there is the knowing that God is ALL and the quintessence of profound peace, stillness and love.

Can you consider life as nothing more than a continuing process of change ?. Who we are is Life – and we are Life Itself. What is Life? It is a process, it is an unfolding, or what we call change. Everything in life changes all the time – and Life is change. When we put an end to change, we put an end to life. Yet we cannot do that, and so we create a living hell, trying to do something we cannot do, trying to remain unchanged when Who We Are is change itself.

Watch nature and let it teach you acceptance of what is and how to surrender to the moment. Let it teach you being. Let it teach you integrity - which means to be One, to be yourself, to be real. Let it teach you how to be natural – how to live and how to die, and how not to make living or dying a problem.

The first and simplest way of looking at relationships is that whatever is within you is what you will recognise most obviously in the people around you. Whatever beauty and love you carry, whatever pain and aggression, you will readily recognise that in others. This perspective is based on the concept that we are most accurately aware of that which we most intimately know.

It is not necessary for us to repeat patterns of painful dramas simply because we have not released the past. The only way to end this vicious cycle of suffering is to become clear, to understand the connection between our level of consciousness and the life dramas it creates for us to live out.

When spiritual interest becomes spiritual commitment one discovers that it can be arduous. One discovers that to be authentically one-with-Self, one has be fearlessly honest with oneself about oneself. One has to lose that which one "thinks" you are. One has to let go of the illusions that you have about yourself: how talented you are, how intelligent you are, how beautiful you are, how successful you are. One has to let go of how special you are and also how depressed, stuck, ugly and unloving you are. One has to loose the illusion that you are not special. In this renunciation one discovers ordinariness and humility which are the best companions on the inner path.

Reminders on the Inner Path

When we attach ourselves to somebody or something we adhere to the nature of the ego-mind, which is to personalise, to own, or to claim exclusivity. Because everything and everybody changes all the time - attachment and the expectations that it brings - causes disappointment, loss and emotional pain. What does it mean? In spiritual work it means don't hold on to anything - experience it, enjoy it, love it, share it, but don't claim ownership. As one cannot claim the open sky, stars or sunrise as one's own, one cannot claim to own anything else. Ownership is the child of the ego-mind's illusions of separation and competition.

Consciously or unconsciously, the meaning of life is the meaning you give it.

We do not reach our highest potential by denying our own humanness. To be human - to experience our own humanness fully - is to be AVAILABLE to ALL of life, and it is what we have been created for. Our task then is to honour our humanness and all our feelings; including the messy ones, the growing pains, the challenges, the aches – it is all part of why we are here.

Your authority lies within.

When aware we can choose to be happy instead of sad, and we can choose to be calm instead of angry. Here is a big secret: we can choose the meaning of something before it happens, just as we do after something happens. Thus, we can create our experience, not simply experience it. Once we accept the responsibility of being the creator of our own reality we can never be a victim again. We become the captain of our own ship and Life becomes an adventure.

If I tell you that everything in life happens spontaneously, despite of you, how would you feel about that?

Humility affords us self-honesty. When we are self-honest we are not prone to having our feelings hurt or "having a bone to pick with others". Honest, self-insight has an immediate benefit in the reduction of actual, as well as potential, pain and suffering.

Spiritual growth is hastened when we willingly accept that we are LIFE Itself, unfolding moment by moment.

Life is impermanence, the endless arising and passing away of everything.

Reminders on the Inner Path

The more we blame other people verbally or in the mind and the more we complain about people or situations, the more we are trapped in the patterns of the ego-mind. The ego-mind loves blame, complaints, judgment and criticism. Every time we fall into one of these patterns the immature ego is exposed because it is obvious that when we complain about something or someone - who they are or what they are doing, should have done, or always do - the more we give power to our "superiority", which is an illusion of the ego-mind. The more one complains the more immature the ego is. Our work, our challenge is to be present in every human interaction and to be receptive to the reflections of ourselves that are available. In this availability, focus and energy can be placed on what needs to be done or what the solution is to a particular situation, instead of engaging in endless ego-stories and games.

Life/God/The Universe has no agenda with us. There is no particular, set outcome for our lives. We create our own reality, our own journey a moment at a time.

For lifetimes I went everywhere with a longing for You in my heart and in my eyes. Then with certainty I knew that there is no You and no me. In the space between You and me, I lost the self, the me, the i. There are no thoughts, no words, no understanding, that can begin to describe the stillness, the knowingness, the vast, unlimited inner sky, of the Self.

As far as inner transformation is concerned, there is NOTHING we can do about it and we cannot transform ourselves or others. All we can do is to create a space for transformation to happen, and for grace and love to enter. The space for transformation is created through AWARENESS. If there is anger, if there is disappointment, if there is jealousy, defensiveness, the urge to argue, the need to be right, an inner child demanding attention and love, or any emotional pain of any kind - whatever it is, be AWARE - fully know the reality of the moment! In awareness, change and transformation happen automatically. All we need to do is to accept and allow THIS MOMENT. In time we realise that THIS MOMENT is where life happens.

Everybody is doing the best they can at all times. A deep understanding of this affords us the compassion to relate to ourselves and others from a different place, knowing that nobody is "bad" or "wrong" but merely doing the very best their level of consciousness allows.

The desire to change anything has fallen away and there is a deep realisation that nothing can be changed anyway. Life unfolds as it unfolds and our task is to EXPERIENCE it. In our availability to life - all of it - we learn and grow as more of REALITY becomes available to us.

Freedom is the highest value of the human experience, even higher than love. Love without freedom is not love. Freedom does not only mean the freedom to do right - if that was the meaning, what kind of freedom would it be? If we are free only to do right, then we are not free. True freedom implies both - to do right and to do wrong.

We are all born with inner wisdom or inner intelligence that is far more intelligent than the human brain. To live our highest potential, we have to discover this inner dimension and then learn to trust and live from it. The intellect can then be used for what it was meant for - logical tasks – and not for decisions and choices.

Everything in creation has already been created and we are experiencing the outcomes and results that we are able to choose, given our understandings and perceptions.

The sun that rose this morning is not the same sun that rose yesterday. From one sunrise to the next much changes - the whole sky is different, the whole cosmos is different - everything has changed. In this insight lies the wisdom of learning to relate to life in a fresh, authentic way in every moment. Not to rely on the mind and its fixed interpretation of what is, and not to rely on the illusions that it creates.

There are no ready-made pathways to inner peace. Inner freedom cannot be reached by following in anybody's footsteps. Inner peace is waiting for you – and only for you - because nobody can "get inside you", and you have to find your own way to get there.

Being ordinary is your real home. Discovering your ordinariness is one of the most extraordinary things that can ever happen to you. It is your birth right. That is why you are here.

The self-imposed stress of many life times - of having to get somewhere to live the highest possible human experience - is no longer there and in its place is the 'knowing' that existence is an eternal mystery that cannot be understood or solved; only lived moment by moment. There is the realisation that life is simply a series of moments without any goal and just living these moments is what it is all about.

The spiritual search is as illusory as any other search! Searching itself is illusory because it takes for granted that something is missing - and nothing is ever missing. All people are searching for the Ultimate, the Unchangeable - God! The Ultimate, the Unchangeable, already IS. It is not distant at all, it breathes as us. It is not THERE, it is HERE. It is not THEN, it is NOW. It has always BEEN us.

Life is a miracle and if you live in wonder you will be able to celebrate no matter what! So don't live in knowledge, in the mind - live in wonder and from the heart. You never know what the next moment will bring! Every moment is new and anything can happen! Exciting!

Within all of us there is an eternal, archetypal Mother, whether we are male or female. The innate ability to care, nurture and protect is a potential that has always been there and always will be there. It is available in every moment, in every action, in every relationship. It is our task to remember it and live from it with awareness. The challenge is to allow our "ability to mother" to shine through in our relationship with ourselves, in everything we do, and in every engagement with every person, animal, tree, insect, river, etc. that is in front of us - and not only towards who or what we single out. Realise deeply that when we care, nurture or protect selectively - it is not our Mother in action but the ego-mind working an agenda.

What we intend is ALWAYS happening - but what is happening may not always be what we anticipated. How is this possible? At a physical level (survival) we believe we are calling forth a particular outcome, but at a consciousness level (evolution) we might be calling forth another. So how do we live with this? We do our very best in every moment without expecting a specific outcome.

Vulnerability is the door to a real, intimate engagement with Life, and it means that we are available to ALL of life; the ups and the downs, the hellos and goodbyes, the springs, summers, winters and autumns. It means that we do not defend ourselves against life, but trust it to such an extent that we willingly flow with its direction, knowing that in the end it will ALWAYS serve us. If we don't get that it is serving us at a particular time, well, then in retrospect, it certainly will!

Times of destitution and desolation teach us that Life is never over. Each day, each hour, and each moment is another beginning, another opportunity, another chance to recreate ourselves anew.

On the journey that I am sharing with my friend Ann, I have come to understand that friendship is a most delicate, gradual process that cannot be rushed or seized upon but should be allowed and encouraged to take its course over time. I have come to picture it as a butterfly, simultaneously beautiful and fragile, that once afloat belongs to Life Itself. For now, I am looking at my beloved friend for as long as I can, when I can, not knowing whether she is yet to go or yet to stay, with the deepest realisation that what brought us together does not conform to anything the mind can understand - only the heart that speaks without words.

Reminders on the Inner Path

Beyond the illusion of being separate there is a divine Consciousness. What we are doing in every moment is to either align ourselves with it or not, an inner acceptance or non-resistance is vital for this alignment. All we need is to accept the moment as it is. There may be pain; there may be weakness, disability or discomfort. Those things may be there, and yet the only thing we accept is this moment as it is.

Thoughts fly across the 'sky of my mind' finding no resting place and their numbers dwindle. One by one concepts fall and 'I' is amongst them. Oh, what sweetness the decent into Nothingness. There is no-one or nothing to attain. There is no-one to fail - no-one - only Stillness, Consciousness, Self, God. What has happened? Nothing changed. It has ALWAYS been there. ALWAYS. I AM.

How can acceptance be helpful on the inner path? Whenever we accept what is, something deeper than "what is" emerges. One can be trapped in the most agonising dilemma - external or internal – with the most painful feelings or situation, and the moment one accepts it, one goes beyond it and transcends it. Even if one feels despair or hatred, the moment that one accepts that this is what it is, one transcends it. It may still be there, but suddenly one is in a space beyond the ego where it no longer matters. Remember, acceptance is an inner happening. The outer world should still be worked, but now the action comes from beyond the ego and it is focussed on a solution that will serve all.

Into Stillness

Silence is beyond all thoughts – positive and negative. Both negative thoughts and positive thoughts take us out of the moment. Only by transcending all thoughts can we become aware of the wisdom and the depth of our residing inner stillness.

Surrendering to what is, is the only thing that can give us the love that we search for in other people. Whenever one completely accepts what is, something inside one emerges that had been covered up by the ego's wanting to be loved by others. It is an innate inner peace, stillness, or inner aliveness. It is one's essence. It is that which one has been looking for in the love of others. It is oneself. When that happens, a completely different love is present. It no longer expects others to love you, it no longer singles out a person or a few people as special to love. Love becomes a way of being.

Happiness, peace and stillness are inherent in our nature. It is not wrong to desire it. It becomes a challenge when we look for it outside ourselves when it already exists inside us.

What causes most of our suffering and pain is the ego-mind's perception of how life is supposed to be.

The ego singles someone out to love and makes them special. It uses this person to cover up the constant underlying feeling of discontent, of "not being enough", of anger and hate, which are so closely related. Then inevitably at some point, the person that was singled out, or made special, fails to function as a cover up for pain, anger, discontent or unhappiness, which all have their origin in the illusion of incompleteness. Then, the feeling that was covered up surfaces and it gets projected onto the person that was singled out or made special – the person the ego thought would ultimately change everything. Suddenly love turns into suffering. The ego doesn't realise that the suffering is a projection of the universal pain that is felt inside. The ego believes that the person or object of their affection is causing the pain. It doesn't realise that the pain is the feeling of separation, of not being connected with the Inner Self - not being one with the Self.

Words and concepts are simply road signs on the inward path; it points us to inner peace and stillness. Therefore the word "surrender" doesn't mean giving up - it is a voluntary decision to let go of the ego. In inner surrender nothing is lost but suffering. Surrender points us to our inner wisdom.

Whatever or whoever today brings, it is an opportunity to become more conscious, to wake up from the illusions of the ego-mind. So why not live life as if everything is rigged in your favour?

As long as we have the idea or concept in our heads "I have a relationship" or "I am in a relationship" (no matter with whom) there will be suffering. With the concept of relationship comes expectations, memories of past relationships, further personal and cultural conditions and mental concepts of what a relationship should be. We try and make reality conform to these concepts and it never works, and so our suffering continues.

What if your inner voice that doesn't speak knows a lot more than you do? What if your greatest teacher is right here, right now? Instead of looking outside to others for guidance - instead of always talking - what if, for a change, you listen?

When we look for someone to love us, we are looking for someone to give us something that we can only find in ourselves. The ego then uses the person as a substitute to avoid turning inward and surrendering.

This is my simple truth: There is no need for religion or churches, or for complicated theories, philosophies or ideologies. The heart is all we need; to make kindness a way of living. The challenge is to live from the heart, from kindness, whenever it is possible - and it is always possible.

Reminders on the Inner Path

Whenever you meet anyone, no matter how briefly, do you acknowledge their being by giving them your full attention? Or do you reduce them to a means to an end, a mere function or role? A single moment of attention is enough. Then you are no longer acting out the script of your unconscious conditioning and programming, you become real and a true meeting between you and the other can happen.

Moments come and go. Situations come and go. People come and go. What is important is not to hold on to anything but to make the moment count, and to make the moment meaningful.

To Surrender is to give oneself up to the original source of one's being. We should not delude ourselves by imagining such a source to be some God outside ourselves. One's source is within - give yourself up to it. That means that you turn inward to the source and merge with it. Deeply realise: there are no levels of surrender - you either surrender or you don't.

When caught up in the trials and tribulations of life it makes NO sense to be concerned with questions and answers. All questions, all answers, opinions, concepts and preferences are from the mind. It is a waste of time and energy. If you are interested in transformation, in ending your suffering, turning inwards and seeing yourself is the key.

Awareness means seeing yourself and emptying yourself everyday and every moment. When empty there is NO argument with life, and no fighting. There is a flow, an innocent interest, a willingness to experience whatever is in front of you; irrespective of it being pleasant or unpleasant. You cannot be fully aware and suffer.

Once one drops the search for understanding - once one trusts that all is exactly the way it is meant to be - one becomes relaxed, soft, open and available to life. One stops resisting life. It then becomes possible to experience the miraculous; the gift of being fully alive and spiritually awakened.

There are NO relationships. There is only the present moment, and in the present moment there is only RELATING. How we relate (or rather how well we love) depends on how empty we are of concepts, ideas and expectations.

The purpose of human life is not to be happy but to become conscious. It is through consciousness and through awareness that we surrender when the time comes.

To the ego, love and wanting is the same thing, whereas true love has no wanting in it, no desire to possess or for a partner to change.

Subservience and obedience are two of the greatest human weaknesses because so much suffering is born out of them. It deprives one of intelligence, it deprives one of decisiveness, and it deprives one of responsibility.

The art of awareness, the act of being in the moment is not that simple; to be in the moment, here, now, requires practice like any other skill worth learning.

A neighbour came to visit yesterday and asked a lot of questions about the inner path, and so I invited her for a walk in the autumn garden. It was cloudy as we walked through the flower beds and the trees, with their varying shades of yellow and orange leaves, the birds were singing above us and the scent of lavender was in the air. She asked: "What is the meaning of life?" and I replied: "I don't know. It is right in front of us, moment by moment. We have to open our eyes and see for ourselves." The dahlias stood tall and red in the afternoon light.

The ego-mind and suffering can only exist if one keeps seeking. Seeking means desire, seeking is moving into the future. Seeking creates dreams, fantasies and illusions. The search can be for money and status, power, relationships, inner peace or truth. WHAT one is searching for is not the challenge - but THAT one is searching, is.

Realise deeply that there is NOTHING to reach and nothing to achieve. When one discovers this, one has found peace.

Know that there is NO map for life. Stop assuming that anybody else's life can be replicated – it is not possible. In awareness we become independent and spiritually mature and we find our own way. Understand deeply that this is the only true freedom: living your own inner wisdom.

In every seemingly ordinary moment, a profound depth and beauty awaits our discovery.

Know that wisdom has nothing to do with intellect. Wisdom is the awakening of inner consciousness and the ability to be new and creative in every moment. It does not function from the past with all its programming; it does not react, it responds.

People often say that they find it impossible to meditate or to silence the mind. The perception exists that the mind can be silenced - and yet the mind can never be silent. Mind means turmoil, anguish, non-stop compulsive chatter, and suffering. When there is silence and peace there is NO mind and the mind is transcended.

The turning point when moving from suffering to inner peace is that moment of acceptance - every time. Whatever or whoever the present moment holds, first accept it and then act. Accept it as if you have chosen it, and this affords you the ability to work with what, or who, is in front of you - not against it.

Independence and being self-assertive is simply the expression of your own intelligence. It means that you accept responsibility and you do what your heart tells you is right. You don't do anything that goes against your own inner knowing. Realise this deeply: without responsibility there can be NO freedom. Without responsibility there can be no end to suffering.

Spiritual progress is a process and occurs in so-called stages. In the beginning one learns of spiritual principles, concepts and realities and studies them. Through studying one develops insights into life without suffering. For spiritual insights to have any value it has to be PRACTICED and APPLIED in every aspect of life - this is the second stage. Through DEVOTION, COMMITMENT and PRACTICE, spiritual concepts become experiential realities - the third stage.

One of the most profound and humbling experiences a spiritual student can have is a naked, honest encounter with the ego-mind. Facing the personal lie you think of as "me" and recognising the myth of 'i". Seeing its true nature for the first time can be devastating and overwhelming. Realising that the "i" or lower-self is at the base of EVERY thought, every action, and every emotion and that, in fact, a sense of self is at the base of ALL suffering. Initially, this encounter brings about a sense of helplessness and then a new clarity: NOTHING is to be DONE. Judging, fighting, resisting the ego is just another egoic strategy. In this new awareness, comes a humbling acceptance of what is, and the insight that Truth and Stillness only lies in the heart, and it is only from the heart that the ego can be observed. Peace is made with the realisation that, in time - when readiness is there - grace and love will step in and the ego-mind will collapse and one will at last be free and wake up from that which you are not. Until then, one can be aware in the moment, one can be here, in the NOW as often as possible.

The secret of sustainable change is availability, a YES to the present moment, situation and person in front of you - irrespective of whom or what it is. Acceptance only comes when one has reached an inner readiness, and if and when one has suffered enough, then one is ready. When we are deeply honest with ourselves we are able to see that we cause our own suffering. We see that suffering is NOT caused by a situation but by our own interpretation of it.

Your life story is your ego-mind's identification with the past - a fiction of your lower-self or little me. No matter who you are or what your story is, at some point or another in your life there is the realisation that life as you know it, your story is unfulfilling, and unsatisfactory. What most people then do, is turn to the future because the present is not good enough. The future becomes their focus because of the promise of fulfilment that it holds. They begin to believe that if they have more financial security, if they meet the perfect partner, if their children are happy, once they graduate, they will be fulfilled - their life story will have a happy ending. Unfortunately that never happens and most people die before they are fulfilled. Fulfilment, contentment, inner peace is only to be found in the moment.

Being human means being light and dark, happy and sad, male and female, healthy and ill. Accepting our humanness is part of our spiritual journey. Living our humanness, especially our darker side, without being destructive can only happen with AWARENESS. In awareness we are aware of our anger, disappointment, frustration, etc. but choose to act on it in a constructive way. At times the ego-mind takes over and we act without awareness. In retrospect, we would then see our unawareness and act accordingly to work towards a solution or to heal situations or relationships.

There is no mind as such, only thinking, and thoughts are moving so fast that the interval between them is very difficult to see. When alert and aware, look into the interval and the space in between. You will see no mind. THAT is your nature. Thoughts come and go - but the inner space always remains.

Through the ego-mind we look at life through the distortions of ignorance, prejudice, resistance, fear, anger, avoidance, expectation, resentment, and guilt. In order for us to wake up to what is real, we have to discontinue these ways of reacting to life. This would mean seeing things as they are, and to deal with them clearly and decisively.

Wisdom is found in inner silence and peace, and when it happens, it cannot be cultivated or borrowed - it is authentic. Only then is there an inner knowing, inner clarity and wisdom - otherwise it is just self-deception. And one can deceive oneself for lifetimes, the ego's capacity to do so is infinite.

It is good to remember at all times that the ego-mind does not experience the world as it is but only its own perception of it.

Reminders on the Inner Path

The very nature of the human experience is an experience of duality or opposites: up's and downs, to and fro, night and day, happiness and sadness. A part of our spiritual journey is to accept that everything changes ALL the time. Suffering reduces remarkably as soon as we accept this and stop resisting life and trying to control it in order to be safe and less fearful.

In meditation I sit with my back straight, place my hands on my lap and breathe. The silence is music, and because I have always been a student of Life, I no longer ask books or other people. In the silence, in the music, I listen to the teachings of my inner voice, KNOWING that the entire Universe is inside me.

Being aware and allowing the here and now has the effect that the future is gradually removed from one's consciousness - it is replaced by REALITY. And reality has NOTHING to do with the mind or human intelligence or the future. Reality is experiencing life without being involved, without a personal agenda, being present and being the space in which everything comes and goes. Knowing that you are not the doer, but that you are being done; that you are the glove and not the hand that animates it.

What does it mean to take responsibility for oneself? It means giving up self-centeredness as a way of living and focusing on changing oneself instead of others, the world and life. It means becoming the change that you desire.

Suffering occurs when we want others to love us in the way we imagine we want to be loved, not in the way they are capable of loving us. Love should manifest itself - free and untrammelled. Once one allows oneself to receive this kind of love, one discovers love everywhere and one discovers that love is the ONLY reality. Love cannot be learned and it cannot be cultivated. Cultivated, learned love is not love, but need or fear disguised.

When the Mayans greet each other they say "lakech" which means "I am another you". May we be mirrors of honesty and beauty as we birth a new way of living for all of humanity.

The meaning of life comes through participation and not through thinking about it. You cannot give meaning to life through being a spectator - you have to participate as fully and as totally as possible.

Our original home is where our physical and non-physical realities merge. Throughout history we have called this unity God, Allah, Brahma, Great Spirit, Tao, Source, Beloved, Universe, The Divine, Existence, Life Itself and Presence. Buddha described it as emptiness or nothingness, and Zen described it as Is-ness, Suchness or the Original Face. Christianity describes it as Heaven or the Kingdom of God. Scientists have described it as the Zero Point Energy or a Quantum Vacuum Sea within which everything floats. I like to call it the Absolute. The Absolute is not Christian, Buddhist, Jewish, Hindu, Muslim or whatever beliefs we create around it. The Absolute is fundamentally unknowable, indescribable, intangible, and inseparable from all that is. To grasp this intellectually is to have a kind of understanding about God, but for the serious spiritual student it becomes an experience. It happens when our inner and outer worlds unite and when the ego-mind - with its fear, pride, conflict and suffering - collapses and we come home to eternal inner peace, love and compassion.

How do we learn to live with duality? We learn to live with INSECURITY. The only sustainable security that exists for all humans is the ABILITY TO ADAPT AND FLOW WITH LIFE. This flow is not a passive acceptance or withdrawal, but an active knowing and acceptance of the very nature of creation and a willingness to participate and actively work with and contribute to it.

After the rain late yesterday afternoon, the garden is fresh and luminous this morning. In the newness I saw a rose opening in the early morning sun and it had such an impact on me. If you have the opportunity to be in a garden today, allow it to touch you and allow it to go deep into you. Let it overpower you, let it overwhelm you. Don't think about it, don't say anything, wait. Be patient, be open. Absorb. Let the garden reach into you, and you reach into it. Let there be a meeting between you and the garden. Remember, the deeper the garden goes into you, the deeper you can go into the garden - it is always in the same proportion. A moment comes when you don't know who the garden is and who the observer is. A moment comes when you become the garden and the garden becomes you, when the observer becomes the observed and when all duality disappears. In that moment you will know the reality of the garden, but while the experience is happening don't think and don't talk inside yourself. The inner talk will be interference and you will never know the garden in its fullness, in its intensity and depth.

The more I learn about the truth of love, the more I learn about self-honesty and the less I feel the need to protect, hide, justify or defend any aspect of personal identity, whether light or shadow. As I share my journey, as I hold out my light, it might inspire others to do the same. As I dance with my shadows, perhaps we will grow together.

When there is stillness, when in meditation, one can transcend thoughts and discover eternal inner silence. In the silence, in the joy, in the blissfulness, in the ecstasy, in the godliness, one experiences an immense oneness.

The dedicated spiritual student soon discovers that the intellect can take one to a certain point and beyond that an unlimited inner knowing is available.

When you are thinking, you experience yourself separate from creation because thoughts create a world that you exclusively exist in - nobody else can think the same as you. So the ego-mind and its thoughts are the root of the illusion of separation and with it, suffering.

We are all different expressions of one reality, different songs of the same singer, different dances of the same dancer, different paintings of the one painter.

You ask me: "what and who is God?"
I ask you: "what and who is not God?"

Life unfolds of its own accord and does not need commentary. The habit of editing and having an opinion about what is witnessed comes from the ego-mind and should voluntarily be surrendered moment by moment. See how compulsively the ego has an opinion about everything and everybody.

It is impossible to be bored in the moment - there is just too much to EXPERIENCE. There might be nothing to do...but there is never a moment when Existence is not unfolding. This unfolding is ALWAYS available and noticeable through the body and being in the moment means that the body and its senses are alert, attentive and sensitive. And in this alertness one is constantly amazed, thrilled and perpetually in a state of adventure.

Among us there is a lot of variety, but that doesn't make us separate. Variety makes life richer – a part of us is elevated in the peaks of the mountains, a part of us submerged in the depths of the ocean, a part of us blossoms in flowers, and a part of us sails in the clouds, soars in the flight of a bird, and sprouts in the green grass. We are spread all over and we are expressed in SO many ways. It means that you can never harm anything or anybody ever again, love and compassion become spontaneous and your very nature. This is Self-realisation or Enlightenment.

Reminders on the Inner Path

The 'noise' of life, or the challenges of life, are not disturbances – they are simply happenings. When we resist them - and when we have the notion that it SHOULD not be happening - it becomes disturbances. When there is an inner acceptance of whatever is in front of us, it comes and it passes.

Total living means being fully alive. If you are angry, then own it and be really angry without acting it out. Be authentically angry and complete it! What do most people do when they are angry? They deny it, smile, or blame others and, in doing this, the anger is not completed - it stays and it waits for completion. It becomes mental chatter and at a later stage it surfaces again.

One basic law of human existence that influences everything we ever experience, is that of completion. Anything that is complete collapses because there is no meaning in carrying it forward; anything that is not complete stays, waits for its completion, and shows up in your life again and again until completed. The mind's obsessive chatter is an attempt to complete that which you have not completed in life. So to find inner peace - to break the constant monologue and discover silence - one's focus must be to try and complete everything that you are doing. When you are bathing, eating, working, playing, relating, complete it. How does one complete it? BE THERE - your presence will complete it.

Whoever looks for and worships God outside of themself has not yet discovered Who They Really Are. The Self is the footprint of all and God is as close to us as we can risk being close to our Real Self.

The temple of the Self cannot be given by a teacher, guru, philosophy or religion. All spiritual awakening is Self-awakening.

God/Life answers prayers ALL the time. Everything we think, say or do is a prayer and produces a response from Life.

We are all sparks of Divinity in the throes of activation and the programming for the process is deep-seated within all of us. It will unfold at its own pace, regardless of steps we might take to accelerate that momentum.

Trust is a confirmation, a "yes". Knowing that Existence is our mother, that nature is our source and it cannot be against us. This means that we trust even when there is doubt - if we wait for doubt to go before we trust, it will never happen. When there is doubt we fall into the knowing that we are always taken care of. What unfolds in our life might not be what we expected, but it ALWAYS, without fail, serves our spiritual awakening.

This world is an experience of great significance but not a place to belong or to become attached to. To be attached to this world is to be lost. The spiritually mature is bound to be detached, an outsider, and even in a crowd they are alone. Even when they relate, they remain separate and there is a kind of subtle distance that is always there. That distance is freedom, that distance is great joy, that distance is their own space. That space is aloneness, not loneliness (there is a difference). The inner journey is a journey of aloneness so let us celebrate aloneness and celebrate our own space. Let our aloneness be a dance!

Our essential nature is peaceful, uninhibited, and spontaneous, and believing otherwise has not changed Who We Really Are. The only problem is that we don't believe this and our disbelief makes all the difference between a life of struggle and one of peace.

One might say that the "goal" of spiritual work is the discovery of the Presence, or of God, not as an entity "out there" but as a radical subjective experience of Divinity within as well as without.

When we are not involved in clinging or rejection, nothing matters. When we do not have a preference, there isn't any need to change what is, as it just is.

This is always my approach: whatever Existence has given me or is giving me, must be a subtle necessity of my inner journey, otherwise it would not have been given in the first place.

The mature spiritual student discovers that NO experience is personal and therefore no preference exists and EVERYTHING can be experienced deeply and fully.

Life itself is our greatest teacher.

In order for us to see our whole self, our true magnificence, we must know our "story" - and then step out of it. To step out of our story we must heal our wounds and make peace with our past and be willing and available to experience the daily struggle of our personal existence. For only when we can BE with our lives can we step out of it.

Modern day slaves are not in chains but are simply lost in the illusions of the ego-mind: separation, competition, greed, fear, anger, blame and victimhood.

Reminders on the Inner Path

If we REQUIRE a certain result in order to be happy, we have an attachment or an addiction. If we simply DESIRE a certain result, we have a preference. If we have NO preference whatsoever, we have ACCEPTANCE. Acceptance is a way of living that is evidence of "a knowing" that, whatever unfolds, is our Inner Divine construction and is a perfect vehicle for moving to higher levels of consciousness; every time, all the time.

To accept something is NOT TO AGREE with it. It is simply to embrace it, whether we agree with it or not, as being the CREATOR of it. This is radical responsibility.

Growth is only possible if there is imperfection and unfulfilled potential. Remember over and again: I am imperfect, you are imperfect and the whole of the universe is imperfect – an eternal, everlasting unfolding of limitless potential. To embrace and love this imperfection - to rejoice in this imperfection - is our quest, moment by moment!

Work plays a very significant role in life. As always, our level of consciousness determines how we relate to work and what importance we give it. When in 'lower' consciousness we relate to work as a burden, an obligation, something that is necessary to survive or might even prefer not to work and to expect others or government to take care of our basic needs (unemployment is higher amongst those in 'lower' consciousness). At the next levels of consciousness work is related to as a means to an end and it is engaged with as a status symbol, to accumulate assets and for power and control (addiction to work could occur). Once aware, there is a willingness to contribute to society and serve through one's work (addiction is still a possibility). When spiritually awakened, one relates to work as ONE of the aspects of life through which one co-creates life and an opportunity to engage with gratitude and creativity, and learn and grow spiritually. Work is no longer seen as an occupation and all work is given equal meaning.

TRUE freedom has a special dimension to it. It is not concerned with the outside world at all - it arises from within oneself. It is freedom from all conditioning, religious ideologies, political philosophies and cultural beliefs.

When in full awareness, solutions present themselves automatically. Indeed, the grandest solution is the awareness that a problem does not even exist.

In the end, it will be found that giving up/letting go of the ego-mind with its illusions and suffering is actually the greatest breakthrough of one's human experience. It changes everything forever in the most miraculous way.

All problems are CHOSEN through ignorance and through being unaware.

A spiritually mature person lives according to her own being. She does her own thing and she does not bother about what other people say or what their opinions are. She does not yearn for respectability, status or honour. She lives her own life at any cost and she is prepared to sacrifice everything – everything, except her freedom. This is what inner integrity is: being nakedly honest with yourself, being authentic and not lying to yourself or others about anything, ever!

In life we fail many times, yet there is no harm in it - it is part of the journey. When it happens, we get up and learn, we become stronger and we vow to become more alert. We make mistakes but are aware not to make the same mistakes over and again. This is how we become wise. This is how the ego-mind matures.

When unaware, you do not understand why certain circumstances or people find their way into your life. You do not know that they are there by your invitation and that you put them there yourself. When unaware, you do not know that you have called every person, place and event in your life to you. You do not know that they are there to create the perfect situation, the perfect opportunity, to 'know yourself' in a particular way.

I am not my name, social status, mind (personality), body, thoughts, beliefs, concepts, soul, role, race, gender, challenges, struggles, creed or religion. I am not part of a social or political identification, culture, new age or nation, nor am I memories (past), personal stories, the universe or a spiritual being. I AM still, silent, formless, eternal consciousness; the unnameable. I AM.

When we live with awareness we can no longer feel that life is happening to us. There is the inner knowing that whatever we are facing at any time, fits perfectly into the awakening of our consciousness. Then, when we experience a life crisis or a challenge, we no longer ask: how do I get out of it, or when will it be done? Instead we know that the only way through it is to be willing and available to be changed because of it.

Reminders on the Inner Path

Our spiritual growth is the greatest gift we can give ourselves and the greatest contribution we can make to the world we live in.

Everything you see is a projection of your particular level of consciousness. When that is lifted to a 'higher' level, see how the same people, situations and scenes change!

The first step to freedom from your conditioning and programming is to realise that you have been conditioned and programmed. In doing so, you begin to be aware of the imprints of society, your culture and childhood experiences on your life today. You can discover that this is the stronghold of your suffering and repetitive patterns. The first glimpse of inner freedom unfolds when it dawns on you that you CAN unlearn them and that they were there in the first place to point you in the direction of your SELF. It is only through your wounds that the journey back home can begin.

When challenged in life do you ask: what is it that I need to learn?

To detach from identification of the self as the body it is only necessary to see the body as "it" rather than "me".

The way that each and every one of us experiences the world is subject to our conditioning and programming, but collectively we create the world that we live in, moment by moment. What we contribute on an individual level is determined by our level of consciousness. When deeply understanding this we realise that there is nothing to blame and nothing to forgive when you know that you have manifested all of your own experiences. Then why frown at those who bring you what you asked?

It is not what you do that counts; it is whether you do it from the ego-mind or from inner peace that is significant.

Spiritual maturity has nothing to do with life experience or knowledge and it does not depend on how many spiritual workshops one has attended or how many spiritual books one has read. It has everything to do with one's inward journey - one's experience of the inner – and the more one remembers and actually lives the silence, peace and innocence of the inner world. It is living one's life in freedom, without considering what others will say. If one always considers others' opinions before saying or doing something, one is not authentic or spiritually mature and still reliant on others for validation. This collective world of illusions that we have created is very strange and insane. If, in this strange world, one becomes alert and aware of one's inner being - of what is REAL - one is truly blessed.

Reminders on the Inner Path

It is important to understand the variance between indifference and non-attachment. If one fully experiences each moment, when the next moment comes, one is able to fully engage with it. There is no need to hold on to anything - this is non-attachment. Indifference may look like non-attachment but is simply the lack of any interest, while non-atttachment is not absence of interest. Non-attachment is absolute interest, but with the capacity of 'non-clinging'. When Life is fully experienced, moment by moment, it is impossible to hold on to, miss something or somebody, or to cling. Enjoy the moment while it is there and when the moment starts disappearing - as everything inevitably does - let it go, move on, flow.

Life is a great adventure, but most people prefer to hold on to the familiar including the past and, with it, the mind. Most people NEVER venture beyond the limitations of the mind and yet one CAN live with such intensity and such adventure that each moment becomes a gift. One must be willing to discover oneself beyond the intellect, for as long as one relies on the intellect as one's only and highest authority, one is imprisoned and limited. One has to discover what is REAL. The willingness to explore one's inner world - and the peace and joy that comes with it - requires openness, courage and a sense of adventure. One has to venture into the unknown and let go of the past, moment by moment; one has to be adventurous! The alternative is to live in an illusory world of comfortable lies.

Every relationship represents not only pain but also opportunity. If relationships energize and magnify patterns and activate the pain body why not accept and work them, rather than try and escape from them?

❧

The moment spring comes, all the trees rejoice and welcome the new season with their green leaves and colourful flowers. Bliss functions in the same way, with our inner flowering that springs forth from the flowers of our consciousness. So, let's not be serious and let's not be sad. Let's be cheerful, enjoying the small things in life, not analysing whether they are worth enjoying or not. The real thing is to simply enjoy everything as it is because, what we enjoy is immaterial.

❧

To turn inwards, to become a seeker of what is Real, and to be dedicated and committed, you first have to become disillusioned with all your worldly desires. At first you have to chase and become fixated on those desires until you see their emptiness. Then you become deeply frustrated and see that they are futile and that whether you succeed or fail, you always fail; that whether you have money or not, you are always poor. When that insight dawns you can really become a seeker of the Truth and the Inner Journey can begin. Otherwise, if you pretend to be a seeker of the Truth, you will bring your whole world with you and with it all your desires. If you are only interested in money, power, status and relationships, it would be better if you do not turn inwards - it is not for you, at least not yet.

The illusion that there is is a centralised "doer" of deeds or a "thinker" of thoughts and a "decider" of decisions is a misidentification and the cause of all pain and suffering of the human experience.

Relationships are sacred and they are the most important aspect of life because it is through relationships that we express and experience Who We Are and who we choose to be. Not merely through our relationships with other people, but our relationships with everything, everywhere. Our relationship with Life, and the elements of Life; our relationship with money, love, and sex, our relationship with trees, plants, animals, birds, wind, air, sky and sea. Life is relationship.

Every act is an act of self-definition. God/Life is the process of self-creation and self-experience in every moment and THAT IS WHAT WE ARE DOING HERE. We are using the experience of that which we are not, in order to remember that which We Are. And yet there is nothing that we are not - we are ALL of it, we are everything. Yet for God/Life/Us to know the part of it that we are now experiencing we must first imagine that there are parts of it that We Are Not. This is the great imagining. These are the illusions of Life.

Life/ God is unconditional and nothing we ever think, say or do can change that. Because of God's unconditional love there is NO one and NO thing that is superior in life. There are NO rankings, no hierarchies and no superior classes or beings - nor are there some who are loved more than others.

Love is an experience, total and complete - it is not possible to love a little, or love a lot. Love is not quantifiable. One can love in different ways but not in different degrees - it is either present or it is not. We are created in the image and likeness of God and therefore, we too, are love. We are not the receiver of love - we are that which we seek to receive. All we have to do to have love is to be love.

Look at what you think you need right now and what you think you do not have right now. Look at that which you feel you MUST have - and then notice, that even though you are without it, you are still here. The implications of that are enormous. If you are here right now - without what you think you need - then why do you think you need it? Sustainable abundance, inner peace and security lies in the knowing that we ALWAYS have what our souls need most to progress.

Since we are a part of ALL THAT IS, it is impossible to be WITHOUT God. When we deeply understand this, we live in our bodies in an entirely different way and WE BECOME FEARLESS. Fearlessness produces its own blessings, for lack of fear creates a lack of anything to be afraid of. Conversely, the presence of fear attracts that which we fear. The way to collapse fear is to KNOW that EVERY outcome in life is perfect. This insight - this reconceptualization - can change our lives for ever! We CAN live without fear, and we CAN experience the glory for which we were created.

Just as there is a third eye, there is a third ear and yet not a lot is written about it in spiritual literature. As the third eye gives us glimpses of our being, the third ear gives us glimpses of our inner voice. When we stop accepting what our outer ears hear as the truth - when we no longer give priority to the opinions of others - we start emptying ourselves from untruths. We start turning inward and listening to our inner voice, and the clearer the voice, the more our steps move in the direction of eternal peace. It progressively becomes stronger and stronger; every inner word leads us closer to WHO WE REALLY ARE. What follows is a deep contentment that nothing is wrong - one can hear and experience inner stillness and one can bless and be blessed by ALL.

Once one has discovered inner freedom, there is NO yearning to be outwardly free. One is capable of accepting life as it is and this acceptance includes that one's outer life will always be a compromise. If one was alone it would be possible to be totally free in the outer world, but we are all interdependent and therefore COMPROMISE is a must.

I believe in God because everything in life is so extraordinary. There is nothing but God. Just be aware of the small things - walking on the lawn when the dewdrops have not yet evaporated; the texture and the feel of the grass against your skin, the coolness of the droplets, the morning breeze, the sun rising - being totally there. What more does one need to be happy? Lying on cool sheets at night, feeling the crisp, smooth texture, as the sheets get warmer and cozier, surrounded by darkness and the silence of the night. With eyes closed, there is only One. What more is there?

As day breaks there is the remembrance that night is not an end and day is not a beginning. Day is flowing towards night, and night is flowing towards day. Everything is simply moving into different forms - nothing ever ends and nothing ever begins - it just changes form.

When you discover that there is only God/Life and its expressions, it will change everything for you.

Reminders on the Inner Path

Yesterday somebody indicated to me that she prefers to be on her own and that she finds it difficult to be with others, sometimes even with her husband. My answer to her: do not renounce the outer world but rather be in it, take its challenges, accept its dangers, its hurts and its wounds. Go through it and don't avoid it - don't try to find a shortcut to self-realisation because there is none. It is a struggle, it is arduous, it is an uphill journey, but it is how one reaches the peak. The journey creates the peak. Self-realisation is not the end of the journey; it is created by the journey, step by step. So never miss an opportunity of living, of being responsible, of being committed, of being involved. Face life, encounter it, and then slowly, gradually the journey proceeds. Yes, it takes time and it takes a lot of work, but nothing in the third dimension (duality) happens without effort. It has to be created. In life, as we know it, nothing is for free and if one does, it is worthless. We have to fully participate in life - awakening and self-realisation do not happen any other way.

We become spiritually mature the moment we start loving and giving rather than holding on, or hoarding. Then we start overflowing, sharing and imparting. The emphasis for the spiritually immature is totally different and is focused on how to get more. With the spiritually mature the emphasis is on how to give - how to impart more - and how to give unconditionally. The giving is a state of being and does not depend on a person or a circumstance. It is like having so many songs in one's heart that one just has to sing them - whether anybody listens, or not, is irrelevant. Will you sing a song today? If so, what will it sound like?

When one lives in the moment - now and here - one is not cluttered with the past or the future and one remains unburdened. One has no baggage to carry and one moves without weight. One is no longer affected by stories and drama. In fact one doesn't walk, one flies. One has wings.

When you feel hurt or disappointed, be alert. When you feel angry and frustrated, see yourself. When you are feeling sad and depressed and when you feel that life is not worth living - those are the moments to be very watchful. When you are surrounded by a dark night, remember your inner light. In time, all these life situations will prove to be very helpful on your journey to higher consciousness - they are meant for it.

The nature of the mind is to want more - more fun, more clothes, more friends, more love, more youth, more health, more money! There is no end to the need of the mind, simply because it exists within the Illusion of Need. When unaware, the mind just pushes further and harder and it does not appreciate what it already has.

Anyone who deeply understands what enlightenment is will never be satisfied with anything else.

The hold of the ego is weakened by acceptance, familiarity and compassionate understanding. In contrast, it is reinforced by self-criticism, condemnation, fear and shame.

How does one reach higher levels of awareness and consciousness? Spiritual learnings are self-revealing and they are NOT acquired. They do not occur in a linear progression like logic. It is familiarity with spiritual principles and daily spiritual practices that open awareness and realisation of the Self. Understand deeply that nothing "new" is learned; instead what already exists presents itself as completely obvious.

The mind and its conditioning is the cause of all separation. To think of oneself as a South African, a Hindu, male or female, old or young; is to accept an identity that is opposed to being human. One should simply think of oneself as a human being.

The spiritual student becomes aware that all knowledge is borrowed. The spiritual journey starts in all earnest when there is the realisation that Truth only arises through personal experience. Unless you can claim experience of something, it is not yours.

Radical acceptance means that you have to say "yes" to suffering in order to transcend it. As long as your ego says: "I don't have to suffer, or I will not suffer," your suffering will persist. When suffering is accepted in the inner world, it can be experienced and completed. When it is resisted, it cannot be faced and completion is postponed. Remember that everything in the universe is geared towards completion and suffering too will complete itself sooner or later. Resistance is the one attitude that feeds the ego without fail.

The problem with the ego-mind is not that it is wrong - it is just limited and distorted. While your consciousness is caught up in the ego-mind your experience of life and the world will be limited and distorted.

The beginning of an experience of God/Inner Presence/The Absolute is inner silence. If you really want to hear the inner voice that doesn't speak, you first have to learn to LISTEN. To know that silence, to be able to hear God, we need to come from the heart, and only from the fullness of our heart can we speak with God. We cannot speak unless we have learned to listen and unless we have found God in the silence. Turn inwards and find the silence and in the silence the Presence. That is only the beginning, and in time the good listener becomes a good observer and encounters God in every moment, every breath, every person, every tree, mountain, animal, everything, and eventually the realisation of the miraculous; Oneness.

I used to believe that turning inwards - meditating and living in the moment changes things, but now I know that committed spiritual work changes our level of consciousness - and we change things.

Love is the only religion, the only god, the only mystery that has to be lived. Love has NOTHING to do with the other. A loving person simply loves, just as a living person breathes, drinks, eats and sleeps.

Thinking is the absence of understanding. When we understand something we don't have to think about it.

No matter where you are right now, no matter what you are experiencing right now and no matter what has happened in your past, you can consciously choose to look at it differently - as a journey that is serving the awakening of Who You Really Are. There is no such thing as a hopeless situation, as hopelessness is just a value that you are projecting onto that situation. When in a life crisis, it is not initially important to know how you are going to get through it. What is important is that you decide there WILL be a way, no matter what. There is a voice inside you that doesn't speak. Listen, and allow it to guide you.

The early morning sun flooding the eastern side of the house with a golden glow; the delicacy and tenderness of spring; the sounds of laughter and play from the neighbour's garden as father and daughters celebrate a birthday; the force of the wind that has been blowing for three days and the dust that comes with it; the losing streak of the Springboks and the downward spiral of the Rand - all an expression of Life, of God. God is found in the moment and not in the past or the future. When aware, here and now and truly alive, there is no longer a judgment of what is, just a completed experience and a deep knowing: IT IS WHAT IT IS.

Most of the so-called bad things that happen in people's lives are due to unconsciousness and they are self-created - or rather ego-created. When we are fully aware and fully conscious, drama does not come into our lives anymore as it automatically loses its attraction. When we live in complete acceptance of what is, this will result in the end of ALL drama - inside and outside.

The Garden of Eden is a myth but the story was intended to convey a great Truth. When we have everything - and we do not know that we have everything - we have NOTHING. The only way for us to know what it means to have everything is, at some point, to have less than everything.

Reminders on the Inner Path

To fully love means to be totally naked without hidden agenda or hidden motives - without hiding ANYTHING. LOVE IS THAT WHICH WE ARE. It is our very nature. Love is a state of consciousness and a state of being, not a feeling, a need, or a physical attraction.

Make no mistake about it - enlightenment is a destructive process; a process of unlearning. It has nothing to do with becoming a better person or being happier. It is the 'crumbling away' of illusions and untruths and seeing through the facade of pretense. It is the complete eradication of everything one has imagined to be true.

Life is always changing! It never repeats itself - even if it appears to be repetitious - and it can never replicate itself, it is impossible. So if you feel that anything in life is repeating itself know that this is due to your inability to FEEL the new. A cloud that you see in the sky this morning will never be in the sky again. The sun that rose this morning will never rise again because the whole universe will be different tomorrow.

Love never hurts anybody and if you feel that you have been hurt by love it is something else in you, not your heart, that is hurting.

Freedom from suffering, or reaching Enlightenment, is not acquired or achieved - it is a state of being that presents itself when the conditions are appropriate. Scientific research has indicated that these conditions are of a neurological nature and are brought about through consistent and dedicated daily spiritual practice. When these conditions are there, the eternal freedom from the ego-mind with its duality and suffering is graced. God awakening to God, in God.

Every moment we face the unknown, the past is no more and the future has still to come into being. The future is unpredictable and therefore, every moment we are at the door of the unpredictable. Every moment the unknown is our guest, so why fear the unknown and why have the resistance?

There are two extremely valuable insights that we learn as spiritual students in the course of our inner journey. The first is seeing our personal level of consciousness as the root of all that occurs in our lives. The second is that spiritual progress is a consequence of constancy and persistence, rather than fits and starts of enthusiasm.

Reacting to life means still being caught up in the past.

The mind is totally unreliable and it cannot be depended upon at all. It is not able to be consistent and its performance is sporadic as well as erratic. It will forget to take the keys, forget telephone numbers and addresses, and be the source of irritation, frustration and annoyance. Furthermore, the mind is influenced by emotions, feelings, prejudice, blind spots, denials, projections, fears, regrets, guilt, worries, and anxieties. It is also affected by fears of poverty, old age, sickness, death, failure, rejection, loss and disaster. All human suffering is embedded in the identification with the mind as self. Realise deeply that you are not your mind - you just have a mind.

Nothing in life happens by accident; there is perfection in the very design of Life. Therefore, nothing happens in life by mere luck – NOTHING – and NOTHING takes place without producing the opportunity for real and lasting benefit to us, NOTHING AT ALL. The perfection of every moment may not be apparent to us yet but that will make the moment no less perfect and it will be no less a gift.

How can we be certain what the eternal Truth is and who is speaking it? The answer: There is no absolute Truth. All that we have to know is OUR Truth and not somebody else's. When we understand this, we understand that what others are saying DOESN'T have to be the Truth - it only has to lead us to our own Truth (and it will do that). When aware, ALL things always lead us to our innermost Truth. Life is Truth revealing itself to itself.

Life is God experiencing itself.

What is the place of humility in spiritual work? It is the acknowledgement in every moment, every situation and every relationship that there is something that one does not know; the knowing of which could change everything.

"Need" is when we imagine that there is something OUTSIDE ourself that we do not have and which we require in order to be happy. When we believe that we need this or that, we will do almost ANYTHING to get it. We seek to acquire what we think we require and most of us seek to acquire this by TRADING. We trade what we already have for what we seek to have. Unfortunately, this is the process most people call "love", but understand this deeply: WE ARE WITHOUT NEEDS! There is nothing we need in order to be perfectly happy - we only THINK there is. Our deepest, most perfect happiness will be found within and once we find it, NOTHING exterior to the SELF can match it, nor can anything or anybody destroy it!

Choosing to be aware and self-honest means that one chooses to say: "I will create no more suffering for myself, or for others and for the world."

Reminders on the Inner Path

Most people believe what others say about them. Subsequently they change their behaviour and belief in who they are in order to change others' perception of them and what they believe about themselves. Most people literally experience themselves through others. How does one stop needing affirmation from without and find what one requires to be happy within? ONE GOES WITHIN. To find what is within, GO within. If one does not go within, one goes without!

Trust means not expecting a particular outcome but rather knowing that whatever result, it is for our highest good. The beauty of not needing a particular outcome frees the subconscious mind from all thoughts about why we can't have a particular result, which in turn opens the path to the result that was consciously intended. We are then able to 'put things on automatic'. When you face a challenge, automatically assume that it will go well and trust that, whatever the outcome, it will be perfect.

This I know for sure: God has NO agenda for us other than the agenda we have for ourself. I no longer live in a paradigm that suggests that there is something God wants us to do and which suggests that God controls, and causes, the circumstances and events in our lives. I know for certain that we control and cause the circumstances of our lives with everything that we believe, say, and do. And, of course, this is determined by the level of our consciousness.

How does one grow spiritually? How does one transform? Only by continuously allowing the new in! One never arrives and spiritual growth never ends. Courage is needed, not ordinary courage, but extraordinary courage. When you allow the new in you can never be the same again; never.

The oak tree at the side of the house is bathing in the rays of sunrise and, because it is autumn, its leaves are falling with grace and beauty. The magnificent tree sways gently to and fro in the sunshine while the falling autumnal leaves dance their way to the ground. The leaves are not dying: they are simply going to rest; melting and merging into the same earth from which they have arisen. There is no sadness, no mourning, but an immense peace in falling to rest in eternity. Perhaps another day, perhaps another time, they may be back and they will celebrate again.

Awareness is about surrender and not fighting. It is an inner happening that results in constructive and positive outer action that allows one to work with the flow of Life and not fight it or swim upstream. It allows one to trust Life.

If you want your suffering to stop, start at the very beginning; let go of the past, forgive and begin again in every moment.

Once the boundaries, created by the ego-mind, disappear there is oneness with everything. In oneness the sun no longer rises beyond oneself and the birds no longer sing outside oneself. Everything happens within you and there is no "without". What more can there be?

With a little awareness one sees that life and death are not separate and that they are wings of the same bird. They are complementary; they need each other to exist; they are inter-dependent. They are part of one cosmic whole.

Seeking, searching is a child of suffering. When in lower consciousness one seeks for material gain, status, relationships and power and one finds all these through 'having'. When one is ready, one starts searching for the meaning of Life: Who am I? Why am I here? One finds one's answers through doing; in books, teachings, workshops and spiritual experiences facilitated by others. Through this one remembers the NOW and one finds that there is NOTHING but this moment. In the moment, seeking disappears and one stops asking books, other people, teachers and the stars and one starts listening to the teachings of the inner voice that doesn't speak. One IS.

Suffering does not exist anywhere in creation but in the human mind. Why? When you relate to life through the mind you never look at life as it is; you look at Life as you are.

My experience is that the more mature the ego is, the easier it is to surrender. A mature ego is trusting, it has confidence and it can let go. It is unafraid and ready to explore the unknown. It is ready to go into the uncharted and it is comfortable with not knowing. When in surrender, there is the understanding that there is no need to fear and that one belongs to Life. Life mothers you. Life has brought you here.

Through awareness and being totally in the moment, our inner-most advice can be heard. There is NO voice - it is simply an inner silence. This is the discovery of the Inner Guide, the Presence of the Divine.

Whenever we say 'no' the ego comes into existence. Whenever there is an inner availability, engagement, willingness and a 'yes', the ego is not there.

We are all One. We exist in each other along with trees, animals, the whole past and the whole future. All that has happened in the world and all that is going to happen potentially exists in us.

The whole journey towards Self/Enlightenment is about how to get unstuck; how to flow with Life.

Reminders on the Inner Path

The purpose of ALL suffering is transformation.

Whether you choose the road to hell or heaven, Existence begins to clear the way and allows you to proceed. To live, is part of Existence, to die is part of Existence, and our ability to choose is part of Existence too. ALL choices are open to you. The more aware you are, the more your choices will lead to happiness, and the more unaware you are the more your choices will lead you towards suffering. The choice is ALWAYS yours.

Whatever you do, make a point to not to do it unaware. Watch every act, every thought, every feeling. Watch and then act and use every moment as an opportunity to become more aware. If you work hard towards it, then when the time is right you become new, silent, peaceful, non-attached and loving. You remain in the world and yet there is a watcher; simultaneously being in the world and not being in it. This is spiritual awakening!

The fearful person can never let go. She is always on the defensive; she is always protecting herself, fighting and antagonistic. When aware, when trusting, she knows how to let go and how to surrender. When trusting she knows how to flow with the river of Life and not against it. She moves with the stream wherever it takes her.

Yesterday I walked down a river path until serenity entered my bones and made me one with the flowing water, the still greenery, the drifting clouds and the multi-coloured flowers. There, between me and the sky, was nothing but silence. In the stillness was the Presence.

Suffering is the process of trying to find happiness, fulfilment, peace and love in the outer world.

At some point on the spiritual journey one becomes aware that there is no need to direct the process of inner transformation through one's intent or actions. For it is one who is directed and not the other way around.

The rising sun; the sweet, wet earth; the sound of the garden and the Great Silence.

When exploring our relationship with the physical body, it is important to learn from nature. We can learn from animals, trees, clouds and rivers. They all teach the same lesson: comparison is the fruit of the ego-mind. One tree is small and the other is tall, and yet there is NO problem. The mind compares and this comparison causes tremendous suffering and pain.

Beyond the ego-mind there is NO superiority; NO inferiority.

Being spiritual students would imply the willingness to risk relinquishing all that we know - including the belief system that defines and constricts our reality - for the possibility that we may experience the perspective of our own expanded selves. It includes the willingness to consider the possibility that all we may value could, in fact, be worthless in a higher sense. That there is any number of avenues to spiritual awakening at any given moment and we know that we WILL get to where we are going by any number of alternative means. By definition, it cannot be otherwise.

Life is a constant re-birth.
Every moment it dies, every moment it is born.

Can Enlightenment or God realisation be given? Can the inner Buddha, Christ, Krishna or Mohammed be created or developed? No, they cannot be created, developed or given - they have to be discovered and uncovered – because they are already there. You just have to reach your innermost core and you will find the inner Buddha enshrined, you will find the Christ, Krishna and Mohammed. God, Christ, Buddha, Mohammed embody the ultimate state of consciousness known to human beings.

There are two kinds of births: the first one is through others, a mother and father a physical birth. The second birth, one has to give to oneself. One has to give birth to one's Eternal Self.

One has to find enlightenment in one's own body; whatever one is doing. It means that one finds the heart of every moment by being aware through one's body's senses. One is the witness of one's thoughts, emotions and body in every moment and at the same time all one's senses are alert. One listens, sees, feels, tastes, senses. In the evening I stretch out on the lawn like a cat, my arms behind my head, looking at the stars, watching the bats and listening to the hoot of the resident owl.

The state of awareness is neither happiness nor unhappiness; it is neither dark nor light, hot or cold. If one feels joy, you have already become identified and awareness is lost. If one feels sadness, one has also lost awareness and one has become involved. The whole art of awareness is witnessing. What will this bring? At the best we can say it brings total inner peace.

What is the one timeless spiritual practice that brings immediate inner peace? Unconditional acceptance of the moment.

Reminders on the Inner Path

Spiritual teachers through the ages taught two distinctive ways of finding inner peace: the path of no-mind and the way of the heart. What then is the way of the heart? One makes a gift of one's life and endeavours to sanctify it with love, devotion and selfless service. ALL of life becomes a form of devotion and worship and one seeks a life of service to others and is uplifted at the same time. Giving is therefore self-rewarding for one comes to experience that there is no 'other' that is being given to and every kind thought or smile benefits the journey of all concerned and echoes in eternity. With the way of the heart one discovers that love is a state of awareness and that full attention is love. On this path of inner stillness, love and awareness meets as one and the same; a way of being and a way of experiencing oneself and others as One.

It often takes us many years to discover that our effort to "fix" ourselves is an endless task and a bottomless pit leading us nowhere. We truly believe that we will be happy if we get rid of the parts of our lives that we don't like, but as we struggle unsuccessfully to rid ourselves of our unwanted parts, we discover that we don't have to get rid of anything at all. Instead, we need to embrace, accept and integrate all of ourselves. In the process, as we mature spiritually, we discover that we are not our past, we are not our body, we are not our mind, roles or life stories - we are that which cannot be named or labelled.

At the root of every thought, there is judgment to either secure yourself or defend yourself. Have you become aware of it? Observe your thoughts and discover it for yourself.

Is there anything we can actually do to end suffering? Some teachers clarify that there is nothing we can do and it happens when it happens. Others teach that effort and certain practices can certainly assist the process of spiritual awakening. What is my truth? My reality is a combination of the two. I believe that there is something that one can do, and yet one is not really doing it. I have realised that there is NOTHING that one can do that is not done by the totality of consciousness. So whether one thinks that you are doing it, or not doing it, makes no difference because the totality of consciousness is expressing or acting through us in every moment. This is true, not just in terms of spiritual awakening, but in ALL aspects of life in every moment. The belief that one is actually contributing comes from the ego-mind and is very helpful at a certain point of one's inner work. In good time, one surrenders to the unfolding of creation as it is. Of course, this too, is also simply the intelligence and love of Consciousness/Source field/God/Life expressing through and as us.

The emotional wounds that we carry become life's teachers that often ask acceptance of the unacceptable.

Reminders on the Inner Path

We can understand only as much as we have experienced; understanding never goes beyond experience.

One of the biggest challenges of the human experience is our addiction to thinking.

Creation, in all its perfection, conspires to give us exactly what we need to fulfil our unique expression. It gives us all the happiness, unhappiness, wanting, fulfilment, addiction, aspiration, trauma and divorce. Every experience of loss and gain and pleasure and pain contributes to an essential part of our journey. Every moment, every day, every experience, facilitates an opportunity for us to wake up a little more; to remember our Inner Presence.

These words like all others in this book contain only my Truth. You have to find your own Truth. To find it in your heart is to know peace beyond all understanding.

Epilogue

The time to write this book and to publish the reminders came as a knowing and once it started, the familiar inner voice spoke without words. It was focussed and inspirational. She was simply the instrument, the channel, the vehicle.

In the process through which the book came about, she realised that again she had changed and that she too had gone through her own process. A new level of knowing; a new level of flowing with Life Itself; a new level of trust was there. She realised that allowing the book to take form through her had changed everything, yet again.

She had come to a place in this lifetime where she had never been before. She had experienced the guidance of inner wisdom with such clarity and focus that it enfolded through her and she merged with it. She had experienced the excitement, joy and connectedness of being in the Stillness and Listening.

The voice of doubt that would plague her from time to time was still. It was replaced by a knowing that everybody has a unique contribution to make in these special times and that the reminders would be her contribution. She knew that in the coming years, as humanity awakens to a new way of living, the contribution of one person will be as much of a necessity as the contributions of the next person and that all people have the same capacity to remember Who They Really Are. When anyone ignores an opportunity to assist in birthing a new civilization - humanity's collective re-birth - everybody loses. When somebody uses the opportunity to wake up and remember a little more in every moment, everybody gains.

Only by turning inward can others be guided. Then a lifetime becomes a sacred quest for the evolution of humanity and the discovery is made that everybody is a learner and everybody is a teacher.

LAKESH.

(Mayan greeting: I am another you.)

www.ingramcontent.com/pod-product-compliance
Lightning Source LLC
Chambersburg PA
CBHW042322150426
43192CB00001B/21